THE DEVOTION FIELD

ALSO BY CLAUDIA KEELAN

Of and Among There Was a Locus(t)

Utopic

The Secularist

Refinery

THE DEVOTION FIELD

poems by Claudia Keelan

Alice James Books

FARMINGTON, MAINE

Printed in the United States

10 9 8 7 6 5 4 3 2 1

Alice James Books are published by Alice James Poetry Cooperative, Inc., an affiliate of the University of Maine at Farmington.

ALICE JAMES BOOKS
238 Main Street
Farmington, ME 04938

www.alicejamesbooks.org

LIBRARY OF CONGRESS CATALOGING-IN-PUBLICATION DATA
Keelan, Claudia, 1959–
The devotion field : poems / by Claudia Keelan.
p. cm.
ISBN 1–882295–46–3
I. Title.
PS3561.E3387D485 2004
811'.54—dc22 2004007435

Alice James Book gratefully acknowledges support from the University of Maine at Farmington and the National Endowment for the Arts.

COVER IMAGE: "Hesiod Listening to the Inspirations of the Muse," circa 1890, Edmond-Francois Aman-Jean. Courtesy Los Angeles County Museum of Art, Gift of Herman and Lila Shickman. Museum number M.86.137. Photograph © 2004 Museum Associates/LACMA.

For Donald and Benjamin Revell

and in memory of my father, Edward Keelan

April 3, 1924–July 11, 2001

CONTENTS

Proem: Day Book xi

1

Airport 3
Freely Adapted 4
Critical Essay 5
In Medias Res 6
The Scarlet Letter 7
Via Negativa 9
Poetry Anthology 11
'Tis of Thee 13
Paradise Lost 14
Hello Beloved 16

2

The Devotion Field 21

3

Southern Anthology 29
You Are My Sunshine, My Only 32
A Poem for the University 33
Documentary for Jack Spicer 36
The Sybil's Afterlife 37

Noumenon 38
Temporal 40
Little Animal Brain 41

4

Phenomenon Nuptial 45
Antique 47
Morning with Boy and Dog 48
Living Elegy 49
Heredity 50
Summer Anthology (Ives) 51
Sun Going Down 53

5

Logo Mundus 57
The First Person (Wittgenstein) 58
My Comrade Gone 59
A Domestic Chapter 60
Ashram 61
Of and Among There Was a Locus(t) 62
Instead of Reading Marcus Aurelius 63

ACKNOWLEDGEMENTS

Grateful acknowledgement is made to the following publications in which these poems first appeared:

American Poetry Review: "Airport," "Antique," "Freely Adapted," "Heredity," "Instead of Reading Marcus Aurelius," "Living Elegy," "Noumenon," "Of and Among There Was a Locus(t)," "Paradise Lost," "Phenomenon Nuptial," "A Poem for the University," "The Scarlet Letter," "Southern Anthology," "Via Negativa," "You Are My Sunshine, My Only"

American Letters & Commentary: "Poetry Anthology"

Bellingham Review: "Temporal"

Chimera: "Logo Mundus"

Conduit: "The Devotion Field"

Electronic Poetry Review: "Morning with Boy and Dog"

Elixir: "A Domestic Chapter," "The First Person (Wittgenstein)" "Hello Beloved"

Five Fingers Review: "Documentary for Jack Spicer"

Gare du Nord: "Day Book"

Greensboro Review: "The Sybil's Afterlife"

Kiosk: "Ashram"

Pequod: "'Tis of Thee"

Smartish Pace: "Summer Anthology (Ives)"

26: "Little Animal Brain"

DAY BOOK

Looked inside An American soul An Amer

I can soul inside

I found An art museum

Where my millions died

Mother Moon Her burning robe

3rd degreeing for the last time

Forgive I read

Before the book erased My moving lips

A box of heaven Sold!

To a rich unloving bidder

I ride next to his chest A chatter

Inside cloth and smell Atomic heart

Muffling The verb auction

What's left us Attached

& adventing

1

AIRPORT

The very young and very old
shall be first and I'm very young twice,
once beyond my own life, thanks Ben,
before I settle back
into the unforgiving
middle, head slumped into a book
mostly missing the sacramental
shoe shine stand, amazing it's still there,
one man who otherwise wouldn't
speak to—gently stepping a shoe into the palm
of—one other who pulls the rag
between his fingers as Bernadette
did her hair, such gentleness and grace
in the scoop and swish and America—
American newspapers &
American boys who see the lamb
and fire

FREELY ADAPTED

In the future
There were blackouts
Pell-mell, *randonnée,* on the beach
And in the bay

The last woman a remaining aunt
Helter skelter *affiché*
And other follies
Along the way

Perpetually beginning
Past afraid

Heh heh over the wire
The sun rises inside a cry

Pell-mell, *randonnée,*
Helter skelter
Hey hey

Bled my gift into the now
To culture citizen's shining paws

Lost the power to withdraw
Endless in change

Controlled hysteria
Earthly fires

Bequeathed
to tradition at last

CRITICAL ESSAY

Anyone writing can come to know
Everything one reading does

Anyone reading might never know
Everyone one writing does

If anyone is really writing
Anyone is really reading

Anyone knows everything writing
Everything anyone reading might never

Anyone for example I I found writing
The experience of the dead gods you

Read in Jane Harrison's *Prolegomena*
The gods dead and gone already in Greece

At the moment Orpheus is born
I for example I found writing the empty

Alpha where the beginning died and I
& Anyone for example Anyone finds writing

Truly writing the end's beginning the empty
Alpha full of the gone God's writing

IN MEDIAS RES

If the house was evenly divided
A bare majority
Must be regarded
A minority
The house was fairly evenly divided
The speeches   & results
The scene   Darkness, though very dimly as yet

A joke
As serious as huge
Concealed the laceration going on within
Let the reader not conclude
Dignity vanished

Dignity vanished

Resolution asked for resolution
For promise   A remedy
Failing that   A third
Who did not believe in principle
Including those in their own person

It was this opened "darkness invisible"
Do not believe in as-far-as-I-knows
They practice nothing   Absolutely nothing
Anbody's speech reading
Sermons to a hunger
Reduced to skeleton

Each actor involuntarily God
Thou   Not thou   Thou

& all such poor representatives of the nation!

THE SCARLET LETTER

> "I don't like it when I find myself responding to what somebody else has written . . . I'd rather respond to something I know nobody wrote, like a puddle . . ."
>
> —THYLIAS MOSS

After I left the scaffold I walked
through the crowd, rights gone,
the texts they quoted yelling after me
meaningless beside my own blood Alpha,
and her fleshy perfection screaming swaddled
in my arms.

I saw my future my Angelhood sprung
from the imagined book of my author

Not the Great American Novel you held sweating
angry inside your incomprehensibility
in high school classrooms

But that tale of choice and retribution
only history, not poetry, could record.

Poetry bounced against the impenetrable wilderness
attempting nature but She was artifice.

She caressed the gaps of my story,
my author's inability to love or to hate me.

I, on the contrary, was free inside
my demarcations and systems,
breath by line by heart by step
leaving the settlement—
You see how it is with me.

Even the hair I tucked
into my cap was a concept,
each sun struck strand hidden
one of the . . . the *ambiguities*
your world continues to hover erotically around,
fingering the silkiness.

"The angle and apostle of the coming revelation
must be a woman . . ." yes,
& I'm achieving Art, disembodied
inside the footsteps

that stepped then into a puddle—
ugh, who wrote *that?*

Shallow, natural hole,
a surface with a mirror,
all the townspeople's looking

crowing out my form
as they gazed in steerage
from that earthly hole.

VIA NEGATIVA

You had nothing you said,
Though all of our life
You'd reminded me that there is no
Such thing as nothing
In nature, so naturally
The grasshoppers drowned in the pool.
It was my job to net them
Until nothing remained
But the shadow of wings on water.

I opened some books and stole some words.
Here, put them back.
I opened a door and stole some air
So—breathe.
No, you don't know what I mean.
I've only seen one movie,
The one where the boy wags
The plane's wing
Over his mother's house
To say he is well,
And encouraged by shadow,
She gives meat and milk
To a young German boy
Who will not thank her.

You think you can get off the movie set?
You better count your lucky somethings.
Some people's lives are, moment to moment,
A live shot of a car explosion
In one of the countries where they hate you,
And the rest of the world, believe me,
Is marching with signs of their approval.

Not everyone loves Jesus or Uncle Tom,
But I do, sweet suffering Christ,
I love them and I love you too,
Generally and specifically,
So march on over here
And let's have some love,

(Put your sign down, I say,
Lay down your v__nity)
You sorrowful monkey, you.

A movie set or an ocean . . .
Sorry to get metaphysical on you . . .
I'm physical about the metaphysical:
Coming from and/or in an ocean . . .
You come too!
And if you insist on staying there,
All alone in your blanket,
Jesus or Uncle Tom or I
(You come too!)

Will rock you in our arms
And the ocean will be your bed
O sorrowful and suffering . . .
The cries of the monkeys on the movie set
So distant now,
We leave our shadows and follow

POETRY ANTHOLOGY

Don't worry about the lost children
They're not lost
No more than you reading this in your underwear
Is it time to go already?
I heard it in the voice of the cartoons
It starts with that kind of exaggeration
& gets louder if you don't shut it off
Don't look for God in the details
S/he ululates in the beetle's wing
You plastered their faces on papers any killer could see
& criminalized their father
Stealing & stealing & stealing y/our love

You complained bitterly about it
wanted to know exactly the smell and taste
            ascribed but you were the problem

Not it

You put it in a frame
You called it the age
There were motorcyclists there
& sawed off shot guns

The motorcyclist fell down
The shotgun killed the teacher.
See what you did?
All the lost children crying under a flag
My country 'tis of thee
My Liberace
In your spangled lees I sing
Perpetua Perpetua In Perpetua
oh mo doh moh doh moh
Art in heaven
WEANED from your name
Gather me the surface turned rote
Gabardine ruined all my care
Because he's been to the desert
On a horse with No
Maine, Henry David and the Indian
Racing with canoes on their heads
Couldn't find Margaret Fuller She drowned
& her baby too went down
My region's asunder
In and out of book and ache and place
Beetled and a black dog
Daddy take your paw
Seeking easy millennium
Oh the mass
Oh the mass
Oh the masticating maw

’TIS OF THEE

The pictures took over
& time was film
No music   Only Flags
I heard their waving
By the plum’s furry blight
Oh early dawn
Mid-day   *Aprés midi*   All day   Every day
Our lady of the shopping cart
Peering through the wire link
Search the depths for a map:
My country for a map!
Where the proper road ’tis a horse
And a dog who sniffs
Out the killer hiding under a bush
Pinning a note upon him which saith:
“The truck stops here”
Mid-day   *Aprés midi*   All day   Every day
A film around the sun
& “Earth’s Summit” not a found vista
But a meeting
Where the third world
Holds dead stars in their hands
& the Secretary of State
Is “doing our very best”
To get a hold of his emissions
I’m leaking with laughter
Our lady of the shopping cart has a nose bleed
In the film, death entered
The guest room and stayed,
Not a character but a sound,
This roaring in the ears
Which was anthem
As motif gains power, when in the tide
She’s released from the ship state that held her.

PARADISE LOST

The novelist was puzzled
Writing stories after a life
Spent strapping life preservers
To event and character, how small
The grand scale could be, after all.
Africa walking through one door,
The Beloved leaving the room.
She didn't have to be a bull swimming the ocean.
Just a Nora, or a Marilyn in flowers,
Beside the inlet sea.

But the poet, lover of cloisters,
Anti-social genius, a spirit
Navigating the hedges of a public garden . . .
Reading inside your rooms
I am a typist of the infinite,
Writing it and writing it
Even as it says *die*—
See me try to understand,
Fully oceanic
Inside your fourteen-line Arcady.

How big is small, and small big, first, last, etc.
The novel just a bully's story and the poem

The country room
Where you first took my hand,
Insisting that I *knew* what to do.
(What? I still don't know, not
Even the beginning.) Your confidence
A city which made me leave the field,
Stone & earth and earth & stone.
This is Eve here & this is the desert.
The book we were all writing decays in galley,
No sea, field, or even meadow
For which our desert was named.
Freud wants in but there's a lot
Of interference and it's ugly
That oceanic feeling, etc. Why then
I'm a fish gasping for air
I'm sorry   I'm very near
          Why'd you leave paradise in me

HELLO BELOVED

> "When my life is over
> It'll be just as over as hers."
> —ALICE NOTLEY

I thought my body
Was for other uses
A prayer instrument   A music vehicle

Nothing as simple as a tunnel

I played with here there

Traditional, singular,
Tradition of lone-livingness
A singularity vocation vacation
                Trace of

Emily Brontë, Hester Prynne,
others—Not mystic,
Alone and with child (inside the world).

What is kindness for?

Veronica washing his feet

Mary's arms

The erotics of absence

I brought to our love affair

Erotics of *raison d'etre*

My pearl you estranged me

Once, in the tunnel

Close in the mud

Both of it and *it*
There were pilgrims there misnaming
Something caved in

A lot of scrambling to the surface
Your face

I wonder if you can tell me, Eva Peron,
Why when the crumbling stopped
It was the waiting
Yes, in the terminal we used
To dig out?

Once thrown a rope
Mistaken for a basket
No One was happy
In her homemade house of reeds

No One misses the point

But the stars above her head
Pointed everywhere
& looking she saw crushing
Grief past, demarcations
Strewn and uh oh

I missed a lot
Never except in seconds
Loved specifically
Accepted an exit role
And called it nature

I'm not grateful for
What bullshit—The Grateful Dead
(Neither are they)
That's what my childhood rolled into
Gave up dope
But won't turn in my hackey sack

Kicking inside the Godhead
Kicking inside the work
Instead of—I don't know—
Existence—But then
I was placed outside at birth
So were you—Erotics of definition—
Existence and ecstasy
Derived both from the same root,
e.g. instruction: "to live"
Is to be outside
Of now, this body,
Whatever noun you want
To place on *it*.

I fell
In love.
Stood back up. Married you.

2

THE DEVOTION FIELD

1.

Body passes
Into another kind
Of body.
Heat, cold,
Contact of the senses,
Come and go.
The body is: body dies.
Its wonder
Within all living, never
(In) for any One.
Opens a door.
Frees the pairs

2.

The wind turns
Mind, a raft,
A blazing fire
On Earth.
Author doing nothing.
Breathing, sleeping, speaking,
Opening or closing eyes—

A leaf unsettled on water.
The city of nine gates
Gave me these dreams.
The light and darkness,
Dream.

3.

Senses are wombs.
They begin: they are
Already, here on earth,
Here and hereafter,
The author
Of presence.
The spot neither high
Nor low.
A spot with skin,
A cloth with grass,
A windless place.
Spring
Little by little.
The mind
Missed both lives,
Caught
In a broken cloud.

4.

A leaf, a flower:
My face is equal.
Turn from it.
Innumerable mouths, eyes, suns,
Outside of peace,
Mothlike,
Bodying forth,
This world.

5.

The field is what knowledge is.
Everywhere are hands, eyes, feet,
Separate lives.
Inside you everybody
The single sun illumines.

6.

Some suffer thinking they are good.
A remedy lies in examining motives.
If you see your will
An arc spread across a plain,
And you see where the points of the arc
Do not touch the plain,

You will understand your goodness is incomplete.
Suffering an air inside an air under the arc.
Breathless, you see the plain is empty,
The arc an arrow independent
And connected to the trace
Where the other stands,
Mistakenly forgiven.

7.

A new age begins
In its dissolution.
Thence the many
Are the forms
Undying.
Understanding shines through
The door: the body
Gold, mud and stone.

8.

There is a fig tree,
A song I know
Whose branches are buds
Rooting into the world.
Its end and beginning
All of nature known here.

Sharpen the ax.
There are no future births.
Shall the sun lend any light?
Part of myself,
The garment of flowers.
Light in sun
        in moon
        in fire.
Become the moon.
Flame in all hearts,
The teacher.
Teacher harms no one
Forgives, in/and/of,
Birthright.
Nature leads to/
Or nature leads to:

9.

"I wanted this and today I want that."

10.

Today has three doors,
Is of three kinds.
A gift given,
Not *because* of

Or *in* of,
But because it *is*
To give.

11.

Walk through the doors,
An *I* in an *of*—
Even if *in* seems imperfectly done,
Do not give up imperfectly.
For now is fire in smoke,
Your dearest loved one,
A pulse in every creature.
This wheel round upon,
I chose and love.

3

SOUTHERN ANTHOLOGY

& sometime later I am on an airplane
Thinking about prison narratives,
How very attached one can become
To prison narratives,
Since, in all I've read, the release
Is assured from the beginning
Or at least by page thirty-six,
There is the eventuality of release
And the poignancy and good humor
Of the prisoners, incarcerated unjustly . . .
They are freer than we are, dear,
Staring at the pine trees
In the piney woods in Alabama,
Planning the future and the old age
We know will come with it.
I wanted to be a red lake
And I was for a while,
I was a red lake and people
Told stories, even myths sometimes
Over picnics by me.
And then *poof,* I was listening to the radio,
I *was* the radio, in 2003
& the announcer spoke politely

And it had come to pass
That in forty years segregation
Was virtually the same in the Northeast
And the West, though not in the South
Anymore, as in 1963 & Selma &
Birmingham and all the holy lands
Of the dark and piney woods clustered near red lakes . . .
Fog came into the prison then
Fog, as they say, a thick carpet of it,
Though nothing like that, just fog,
A cloud chamber, a spate
Of time under pressure of air &
Water and voices all speaking
In one, twanging, incomprehensible language—
Oh Sophia cried.
Oh Sophia spread her hair
Across the dark skyline
And cried.
"Though I am gone," she said
Through her gelatin tears, "though
I am irremediably gone (for now)"
She said through her glycerin tears,
"The world will continue its craggy story
And I will hope you hear it
From time to time."
The snow winked happily in the snow mound.

And "the mound" in Tuscaloosa
Sinks suddenly away from monument
Into the earth, Black Warrior
Shedding his name.
The prison door, too, has avoided monument.
I touched it but was not allowed to enter
& as surely as Martin left the urinal
And narrow bed, his speech in hand,
Left for his eventual assassination,
We left the museum
And walked out through the narrow door
Into the possibilities of the next page,
Or more nearly, another day.

YOU ARE MY SUNSHINE, MY ONLY

You are my sonshine,
my lost Shoshone,

I skin a *beau fleuve*
in your heart

If there is tripartite,
I can't be sure dear,

Another name for *deer*
is *hart.*

A judge lay weeping,
his robes were skewed, dear

His robes a Buff'lo
inside a park.

Inside the hair, dear,
the missing part, dear—

He turned to bread there
and there, he died.

A POEM FOR THE UNIVERSITY

1.

We were prepared to love you
Mistaking the monastery
For the master's footsteps,
So silent and so gone now.
You were only a boot
On an untethered animal
Grazing in *Veritas* pasture,
Near those trailers where you housed
Passion & Ecstasy,
Your part-time instructors.
Oh, but those in the highest robes,
In the throes of the Holy Orders:
The Woolf scholar,
Pulling Virginia still down,
Down into the river,
Ophelia sister, wishful incest;
Or New History,
Making you pay with her hands of ash;
Dr. Poetics, fleeing Mao's ghost inside the end of English,
A suicide himself,
In the fur coat of the Republican Party . . .

Prithee, Prithee—

Could it?

Marry! Zounds!!

Oh—

Drink to me only with thine . . .

& I will & I will pledge . . .

"Apocrypha."

"David Herbert Lawrence was born in Eastwood, Nottinghamshire, in 1885, fourth of the five children of a miner and his middle-class wife . . . His first novel, *The White Peacock*, was published in 1911, just a few weeks after the death of his mother to whom he had been abnormally close . . ."

So what was her middle-class name?

2.

Flies in the flowers, not even bees,

In the petals and not the middle,

Teaching periphery.

How far we've come—

How far by the dawn's early

Edging, by the ramparts

We watched gleaming,

Under water, under pages,

Heavy pages, heavy lettered pages . . .

Entre nous: Everything

Entre nous.

At bottom one voice:

Ula Zion *Ula Sodom*

Ula *Ula . . .*

Tethered between Our fancy animal,

& yellow universidad,

Our brain drops letters . . . From here they look like:

Love, Prophecy . . .

Of this immediate present . . . Flies, not bees,

Poetry in its petals, its windlike transit . . .

Poor brother dog,

Always in the middle

Of perpetual dog song.

Love, Prophecy . . . & a collar tied to a chain.

3.

The anthem stops. The motors recede.

Entre nous: one after the other . . .

To the top of the hill, to the top of the hill!!!

& Gethsemane & Golgotha,

One hard after the other . . .

Pick up the torn curtain.

At the murdered end: *Love, Prophecy.*

A book.

DOCUMENTARY FOR JACK SPICER

Don't rise for the dream.
A walrus, dying for hours in a frozen ocean,
Nanook straining on a rope from shore.
Its mate straining from the water, tusks locked.
A walrus/an extinct man dragging a dead walrus,
And an abandoned igloo just before dark.
I saw Austerity and I called her name.
That was not her name.
She stood outside,
And there you were, in deep turmoil,
& still had them all laughing
& exactly two months later you die.
So the walrus is everywhere:
tusk
Though no, that's only a girl lying,
Lying sideways on the floor.
And though there is only snow justice in the snow,
I want to take her hand,
Pull her towards me or to her feet,
But the day is in dream and she does not rise.
People are starving.
Nanook's family has forgotten the camera.
Pulling off fur boots & pants & coats
(Something large has swum away)
They put their shoulders together, and sleep.

THE SYBIL'S AFTERLIFE

a poem for Ronald Johnson in heaven

There's a hole in the beam,
31 December, 1999.
Sight can't be taught.
The angels the century boys adore
Are sitting, yes, standing, yes,
All over the place.
I shut the door.
Feel the ending.

Inside the sight and therefore not fable,
I made them leave the room.
This is my book.

Inside and on the surface of my face,
All that mistaken love,
Gone now so you can see just how
Empty. Empty possible zero.
Auld lang. I met myself and left
With me & she came home forever changed.

NOUMENON

Our son fell to his knees,
Ben someone else now, someone—

The dust I write in,
The closet exhorted for prayer.
But I didn't enter,
Not today, not all day.
Culture's confessions arrive in the mails.
Yes, they're lost, so many,
Piled on the kitchen table,
Their faces age progressed.

The end of the century wants to be faithful to time.
Someone is watching the wind believing erasure is Truth.
Earlier, someone fingering the years spent,
Tastes her eventual death in the dust that spins
Off the book she is reading.
Now someone some
Would call the same someone,
But not the faithful to time,
Is summoning
The new forms from the air, but no—
Someone draws blanks.
Someone in her heart, Celan

Shoving Jabès' *Book of Questions*
Back through the mail slot.
The sound of it hitting the floor.
The lost original in the story of the clown.
Together once, when we walked we cartwheeled,
But joy made pride and we were severed—

Are you my Ben, are you my first
Trying to fit himself back to
The someone now everywhere.
Sorrow's learning loved Her all.
His namesake shot on the border hours,
His other name, including two wives and the donkey,
& the first brother confined to the wheelchair.
Someone taking tickets at the bridge.

First and last,
Following the dust of your reading.

TEMPORAL

There are deadlines
that won't be met
until it's over.

Each thing finished
moves quickly to the next,

Proving soul is not pathology
but nature.

Not the genre, but the trembling inside
all living:
                    I saw the hollyhock sprout
                                        then turn to light.
I see you each week,
praying to the dog food and soil,
to the dust and bits of paper,
making a sign to each
before you get in the car to leave.

Not what we can know,
but what we can do.

Carrying your wave inside us in the dark.

LITTLE ANIMAL BRAIN

Little animal life
You desert me
A bird in an empty shuttle
Can't land by earth
Or by sea
Fly away now
Soul's protocol

4

PHENOMENON NUPTIAL

The ring sits on a box and she doesn't know,
She can't remember who put it there.
Dust falls on the box, she sees particles sometimes
Too minutely, each speck
Translucent in morning, and at evening's end
When the sky above the Spring
Mountains is red from the same dust—
The time when she's embarrassed, or shy,
More closely—of its hue, shy of it,
Shying back from red
The color of prehistoric clay
Making its display above the neighborhood,
If you can call it that—offering its display,
Its adornment—so adoring is the sky
Of its color, there above, to the four houses
Set by themselves in the desert.
Shape itself frightens her, no—
It's only embarrassment, or shyness, or fear—
Only the ring, for example,
Lying in the dust on the box there.
It scores its roundness
Into the wood, the dust complementing
Its purpose, falling all day down around
The simple, gold band when she—
She can remember neither when she took it off,
Nor who put it there, on the box
That held some books, *The Scarlet Letter* for one,
And *The Blithedale Romance* for another.
Their ambiguity, or Hawthorne's,
More closely . . . He knew about shape
-Shifting, Hester then Xenobia, evolving
One out of the other and both

Ultimately eluding shape's misery,
Their misery ultimately made mostly
Of the immaterial.

Some moments ago,
When she was thinking again of the ring
On the box, trying to remember the last time
She'd seen it, she'd had to swerve—to shy away—
Full of first fear and then embarrassment,
From the truck she hadn't seen
When she turned left on to the highway,
She and the boy so close to collision
That surely would have led to dust . . .
She'd lifted a shaking hand to her mouth
And bringing it back more firmly
To the steering wheel,
She saw the ring on her finger.

ANTIQUE

She brought the teapot because it was broken
& broken still valuable,
A thing not available to her otherwise.
On its restored surface a pastoral
Flickered once. Too late.
She was not honest but she was a poet
Mending the broken valuable . . .
"What absolute nonsense!' cried the Earthworm. "Nothing
Is ever all right in the end and well you know it."
Poor Earthworm, Ladybug whispered,
Loving all that is disaster
Bellydown breathing with it everafter.

MORNING WITH BOY AND DOG

Repetition denies being.
Something died
I
No longer live
Here.
Here an unfamiliarity I prepared
One morning to the next.
The sun is out!
Not to have prepared "painstakingly"
Is not to have denied it.

You decide what it.

Life intrudes on the page.
All those interruptions to curse and curse?
That's where it lives.

LIVING ELEGY

Inside the sudden and where
Have they gone,
The coffee drinkers and short men?

Tasting apple and Ben
Taking each bite slowly—Cinnamon
Oh cake!   Hurry   We're in space!

Nearly home and the billboard
Men and women, all ages
At the starting line of a race,

We can wait
A patent lie
Brought to you by Palm Valley Memorial Garden.

My father wants to be burned
& I,
I can see his old brown hand
Writing this,
& then I hear the birds in your message.

HEREDITY

I did not die into a new heart.
Dying was the heart
& you who took our son's cut hair
                & sprinkled it among the flowers—

Of suns, flowers are made.
I is there, his hair
spiraling through a flower.

Nothing new, just a purple flower.

SUMMER ANTHOLOGY (IVES)

I was not after all interested
In the reality of the unseen.
The propaganda, the propagandists,
Of Spirit. Spirit *is*, uh-huh.
This is America, I see it.
America is not after all, interesting.
Places themselves aren't interesting.
Seeing is sometimes hearing.
Four boys on a styrofoam raft
In a cove on Ozark,
D'eaux arc . . .
They ride its line
Fishing with bow & arrow
(Dock Squeak) (Wind Blows)
& later they anchor
The boat, tying a rope to the arrow.
America is not after all, interested.
These four boys are interesting
& the American music
anyone hears if she's
Listening (Dock Squeak)
(Wind Blown)
Brown backs and white legs,
The Body Electric, a styrofoam

Raft, arrow's the anchor
& all the other authors here
(Come back to the raft, etc.)
Your life now the (un) loaded
A. not after all interested
BANG! Deerslayer
An arc in their crazy
Paddling—the music you
Hear if you're listening
Well before the 4th of July
(Wind Blow) (Anchor Lift)
America is not interested after, etc.
Floating among the paper
Cups and beer cans,
Vesuvian dives BANG
These white-legged people
D'eaux arc can you see it
Fishing with (Dock Squeak)
No boat to speak of
They anchor, hidden in a cove.

SUN GOING DOWN

The occasions wouldn't stop occasioning—

Occasion for happiness—
For stupidity with her feathered crown—
Occasion for dreaming—
Jack Spicer the best singer
In a salsa band,
& the evil dwarf in mine,
Looking for our bridal bed
In a room named after a towering plant . . .

Occasion for murder, daily,
The nation's transparent plans
Occasioning the bodies of the new soldier
Sportive in khaki and floppy hat,
Wide-spread Kentucky eyes too blue for horror.

Oh occasionally, occasionally—

Times for murder daily
At "home,"
Both army and Islam
Falling bus driver, shopping ladies,
School boy and all
Waiting at the occasional mall.
The occasion a sequence,
A symptom, a
Spate of minutes held
Momently in place by
Bodies, by action, by architecture
By leaving the scene, not finding the room
Or finishing the song; by dropping your pants

& running freely in green-leaf-sand.

Occasion for nightmares not remembered.
For the radio all through the days,
For the missile shot from the Marshall Islands in the Pacific
To implode freely over our home in Las Vegas.
For my boy's terrible crying then,
And the life we shared together
Ending, I believed,
Until news came of the test—
This is just a test . . .
Is it all a test?
My mother thinks so,
Crooning beside the ashes of my father.

Occasion for hatred
For the men
At the Pistol Range,
For the flags smothering their trucks . . .

Occasion for dreaming
Of burning down the Pistol Range,
Of destroying the bulldozers
And cement trucks paving the Mojave;
Of gathering the flags and sewing them
Each to each into a shroud
For a country going down,
In the aftermath of its occasion.

5

LOGO MUNDUS

The gaps   I mean

            I   put them

where?

            To let breath in

            For thee

Love broke the line

            & s/he was free

THE FIRST PERSON (WITTGENSTEIN)

It might be useful to give human beings
Two characters.
Two states lapse
Suddenly one into the other.
Talk of the pair.
The even days
Happened on the odd days,
A composite "person" or "personality."
"Personality" hasn't got one legitimate heir.
"I" is broken.
The wind blows "I see,"
"I hear," "I try,"
To difference.
The recognition of person is an error,
Or an error has been provided.
I see a broken arm
And think it is my neighbor's,
A bump on his forehead
Is mine.
I doesn't choose the mouth which says it:
Something bodiless
Has its seat in our body.

MY COMRADE GONE

Heir no more.
Father went.
Love and skill went.
Poverty joined me.
He never handled a tool
Or a machine in his life.
It cost him success.
He gave me expression.
His name was Edward.
He saw that love had no bounds.
He was a born mechanic.
He was my father,
My hands, my feet, and my eyes.
For a living faith I
Become the loss of one,
His imprints read
On every particle of dust.

A DOMESTIC CHAPTER

As long as the world lasts,
I claim responsibility
For those with me or alone.
The eternal duel
Admits no truce.
The law of love is associated with any.
I like the world,
The present in wilderness.

ASHRAM

Soul wired: "Has departed."
There was no exaggeration in this.
Guru and I had imperfections.
Power conferring on the pupil not power,
And still . . .
If not a disciple, a servant.
I saw "once" for time and time after.
I-in-other embraced poverty,
Shone with glory borrowed from my innumerable.
The world is in need of true soldiers.
Service, service of the world,
Vision of God—
Not separate things, just different.

OF & AMONG THERE WAS A LOCUS(T)

a poem for Bard College

"We ought to say a feeling of *and,* a feeling of *but,* and a feeling of *by*, quite as readily as we say a feeling of *blue* or a feeling of *cold.*"
—WILLIAM JAMES

It may surprise you to know
I'd like to make it perfectly clear
Cars left in the parking lot
Will be towed
It may surprise you to know
Of suns
& flowers
Are's made
I'd like to make it perfectly clear
& survives in midsts
In midsts among and of
That Saturday I was staked out in the parking lot
Of's surprise sunned among the flowers
Wed to clear midsts in and of

**

What strikes me most is how they aren't lonely, so certainly so that when I was among—though not *of,* of that I was certain—them thinking through their speaking, was not lonely in the *of* of my loss to the *of* they were so clearly among—so certainly not lonely, so that I now, not among their speaking, thinking through my thinking alone (as I continue to fail to speak), am placing my thinking on the hollow that is certainly hollow in its hurting where they were of (I let them), & among

INSTEAD OF READING MARCUS AURELIUS

Not the night poem
Not that one
It was morning and the hummingbird moths
Were hunting in the bottlebrush
Not silence either nor absence
But the slow breathing of father and son
The books of others
Tho' not Hannah Arendt
The name she woke thinking
"I need to read Hannah Arendt."
All this before leaving
And more

Pill bottles with her name on them
Little bags of jewelry, of food,
A pen safe in a loop
The still air
And hummingbird moths flying through it
Hunting, he said, in the dawn
An enormous cup of coffee
And the slight unease inside her mouth
—Sharing their material?
Her intentions appreciated by strangers
The morning's rose gratitude

Lodged there, and rising, in her breath
Cerebral cortex there too
Which part of it loved music more than sight?
The hummingbird moths yes
But hardly their bodies (can't see them)
Rather the vibration of their—of what must be their wings?
The darting between the flame-red brushes

And what makes people laugh when they're not happy?
Registering that, feeling a crease on her brow,
Those sounds opposing each other
—Flying moth
—Laughing Lady traveler

The bronze face of the dead man in her lap
Who believed opinion was everything
And was ready to "accept without
resentment whatever may befall."
Falling children.
four out of five dead, except the "worthless Commodus
who lived to succeed his father."
Hmm.
What would Hannah Arendt say
She wanted to know
The beauty of human enterprise, its folly, from above
Greening a desert
The indifference then and the glory
Of the red rocks
The human lines of a freeway
The wind trace on the small mountains
Nothing could live there
No, this a thought limited by a humanist idea of life
All the things she couldn't see
Living there below
Plants never yet classified
Scorpions and floating organisms
and Oh! A river!
The Colorado!
Not reaching its original destination
At last hearing, miles short of it
And its water "misting" the tourists at the casinos
O beautiful   O spacious
Your grainy grains of sand
Enjoying her belly for some reason
Enjoying the blue ink on the page

It's still there anyway, the Colorado
Long and skinny and in a canyon
Not the night poem
The day poem of travel
And people pointing
Thoughtfully chewing her glasses' stems
Not thought   Not fully
Her teeth lightly on the plastic
How relevant! How marvelous and relevant!
She is in love with all the wonderful things
Teeth for example and biting
The floss sliding between the cracks
Smiles and snarls, as on a Ferris wheel
The English professor had said he didn't like those formless things
Speaking of Allen Ginsberg's poetry
And "Howl" the poem she was ready to teach again
All buttoned up with Jane Austen under his arm
And though it is true that candor abolishes paranoia
She did not say "go to hell fathead"
—Allen, dear man, wouldn't have wanted it—
But "goodbye" there on the stairs
Some things are desperate to be eaten
All the fine cereals in their boxes
The egg dishes she either chooses or does not
She's sleeping
The world below is full of rectangles
Farms are spreading across America
Trees come back and buildings
Nothing whispers in her ear
Sounds come in and out and in
She's awake for the second time today
Praise the open eye the awkward hands
The belly digesting the cereal
Praise the seat where she sits
Fly, Fly—Be a moth in your life
Be a quick movement among flowers
Bloom

RECENT TITLES FROM ALICE JAMES BOOKS

Into Perfect Spheres Such Holes Are Pierced, Catherine Barnett
Goest, Cole Swensen
Night of a Thousand Blossoms, Frank X. Gaspar
Mister Goodbye Easter Island, Jon Woodward
The Devil's Garden, Adrian Matejka
The Wind, Master Cherry, the Wind, Larissa Szporluk
North True South Bright, Dan Beachy-Quick
My Mojave, Donald Revell
Granted, Mary Szybist
Sails the Wind Left Behind, Alessandra Lynch
Sea Gate, Jocelyn Emerson
An Ordinary Day, Xue Di
The Captain Lands in Paradise, Sarah Manguso
Ladder Music, Ellen Doré Watson
Self and Simulacra, Liz Waldner
Live Feed, Tom Thompson
The Chime, Cort Day
Utopic, Claudia Keelan
Pity the Bathtub Its Forced Embrace of the Human Form, Matthea Harvey
Isthmus, Alice Jones
The Arrival of the Future, B.H. Fairchild
The Kingdom of the Subjunctive, Suzanne Wise
Camera Lyrica, Amy Newman
How I Got Lost So Close to Home, Amy Dryansky
Zero Gravity, Eric Gamalinda
Fire & Flower, Laura Kasischke
The Groundnote, Janet Kaplan
An Ark of Sorts, Celia Gilbert
The Way Out, Lisa Sewell
The Art of the Lathe, B.H. Fairchild
Generation, Sharon Kraus
Journey Fruit, Kinereth Gensler
We Live in Bodies, Ellen Doré Watson
Middle Kingdom, Adrienne Su
Heavy Grace, Robert Cording

ALICE JAMES BOOKS has been publishing exclusively poetry since 1973. One of the few presses in the country that is run collectively, the cooperative selects manuscripts for publication through both regional and national annual competitions. New regional authors become active members of the cooperative, participating in the editorial decisions of the press. The press, which historically has placed an emphasis on publishing women poets, was named for Alice James, sister of William and Henry, whose fine journal and gift for writing went unrecognized within her lifetime.

TYPESET AND DESIGNED BY MIKE BURTON

PRINTED BY THOMSON-SHORE